Workbook

for

Four Hundred Souls

By

Ibram X. Kendi & Keisha N. Blain

Genius Reads

Text Copyright © Genius Reads

All rights reserved. No part of this guide may be reproduced in any form without permission in writing from the publisher except in the case of brief quotations embodied in critical articles or reviews.

Legal & Disclaimer

The information contained in this book and its contents is not designed to replace or take the place of any form of medical or professional advice; and is not meant to replace the need for independent medical, financial, legal, or other professional advice or services, as may be required. The content and information in this book have been provided for educational and entertainment purposes only.

The content and information contained in this book have been compiled from sources deemed reliable, and it is accurate to the best of the Author's knowledge, information, and belief. However, the Author cannot guarantee its accuracy and validity and cannot be held liable for any errors and/or omissions. Further, changes are periodically made to this book as and when needed. Where appropriate and/or necessary, you must consult a professional (including but not limited to your doctor, attorney, financial advisor, or such other professional advisor) before using any of the suggested remedies, techniques, or information in this book.

Upon using the contents and information contained in this book, you agree to hold harmless the Author from and against any damages, costs, and expenses, including any legal fees potentially resulting from the application of any of the information provided by this book. This disclaimer applies to any loss, damages, or injury caused by the use and application, whether directly or indirectly, of any advice or information presented, whether for breach of contract, tort, negligence, personal injury, criminal intent, or under any other cause of action.

You agree to accept all risks of using the information presented inside this book.

You agree that by continuing to read this book, where appropriate and/or necessary, you shall consult a professional (including but not limited to your doctor, attorney, or financial advisor, or such other advisor as needed) before using any of the suggested remedies, techniques, or information in this book.

Download Your Free Gift

Before you go any further, why not pick up a free gift from me to you?

Smarter Brain – a 10-part video training series to help you develop higher IQ, memory, and creativity – FAST!

www.Geniusreads.com

Table of Contents

Introduction	7
Part One	8
Summary of Part One	8
Questions:	8
Part Two	10
Summary of Part Two	10
Questions:	10
Part Three	12
Summary of Part Three	12
Questions:	12
Part Four	14
Summary of Part Four	14
Questions:	14
Part Five	16
Summary of Part Five	16
Questions:	16
Part Six	18
Summary of Part Six	18
Questions:	18
Part Seven	20
Summary of Part Seven	20
Questions:	20
Part Eight	22
Summary of Part Eight	22
Questions:	22

Part Nine	24
Summary of Part Nine	24
Questions:	24
Part Ten	26
Summary of Part Ten	26
Questions:	26
Conclusion	28

Also, make sure to purchase companion book Summary of Four Hundred Souls by Genius Reads on Amazon

Introduction

This workbook is designed to be a companion to your copy of *Four Hundred Souls* or our *Summary and Analysis of Four Hundred Souls* by Ibram X. Kendi and Keisha N. Blain. The original book is written in ten parts each looking at a different period of history and drawing out key themes and ideas that emerge from a comprehensive reading of the African American experience.

In each part of this book, you will find a short summary of what is contained in each part, with many of the specifics left to the original book or *Summary and Analysis* to explain. We've looked at some of the key learning outcomes suggested by a reading of *Four Hundred Souls* and have created questions to enhance your reading.

In the interest of ensuring you take this history in the context that it is meant, you will not find answers to the questions put forth in this book. This approach is meant to support your ability to absorb the key information contained in the original and help you retain it.

Part One

Summary of Part One

The first part of *Four Hundred Souls* by Ibram X. Kendi and Keisha N. Blain deals with the early plantations in Virginia. It takes into account the ideas of why some of this history is rarely studied in schools and some of the misconceptions about the kind of people that made up the slave population in British Colonial America.

It also looks at some of the early legislation and morals that were raised as the fledgling institution of slavery grew. Finally, it looks at the family and complex relationships that were built or broken in early to mid-seventeenth century Virginia.

Questions:

1. Nikole Hannah-Jones suggests that the story of the *White Lion* has been erased. Why do such historical erasures exist?

2. At this period, many West African nations were rich and highly developed cultures with specific ideas about how cultural history is maintained. What types of people were captured and brought to the Americas?

3. For Ijeoma Oluo, even though her mother is white, why can she never be anything other than a Black woman?

4. What well-known historical character interacted with the tobacco-growing Black woman known as 'Go-go'?

5. What was the role of gender in the Virginia General Assembly Code of 1643?

6. As a freed slave and now a landowner, what concerns does Anthony Johnson have to deal with?

7. What factors influenced the make-up of captive Black families?

8. What was the reward for Black slaves fighting against Indigenous peoples?

9. What does Jericho Brown compare the continued struggle for equality in his poem?

Part Two

Summary of Part Two

Part two of *Four Hundred Souls* by Ibram X. Kendi and Keisha N. Blain takes a wider look at events in Virginia and how the Virginia Assembly accelerated the laws needed to keep captive Africans under control. It looks at the difficulties of the expansion of the slave trade and the rules around family and religion.

It looks also at the wider context of slavery in European countries and early dissent from white people over the morality of keeping slaves.

Questions:

1. What was the outcome of the 1662 Virginia Assembly and what would it have meant for Elizabeth Keye's children?

2. Similar to the 1662 law what did the 1667 Virginia Assembly law on Baptism mean for Black children?

3. Initially, on the whole behalf, did the Royal African Company operate?

4. What were the long-term effects of Bacon's Rebellion?

5. What potential reasons were there for the Virginia laws set up to restrict self-defensive arms from slaves?

6. What were the pros and cons of the Code Noir for enslaved Black people?

7. For what reason is Christopher J. Lebron particular vocal in his praise of the Quakers of Germantown?

8. What paradoxical resource did the Portuguese use when setting up the Transatlantic Slave Trade?

9. What is your interpretation of Phillip B. Williams's poem, and why does it evoke the period looked at in this part of the book?

Part Three

Summary of Part Three

This section of *Four Hundred Souls* Ibram X. Kendi and Keisha N. Blain deals with the start of the 18th century and reactions to the sudden expansion of the slave trade. It moves from Virginia to New York and finally away from the British colonies.

It takes us to places where slaves were able to find freedom, albeit sometimes short-lived, and reveals how African American identities were forged in spite of, and in some cases because of, European power plays and culture. It invites us to look at how the European powers had different ideas about religion and slavery as well as how they began to depend upon slaves as a commodity.

Questions:

1. What biblical story did Samuel Sewall take inspiration from when writing his tract against the practice of slavery?

2. What did the 1705 Virginia Assembly Act mean for Black children?

3. In what area of New York was the municipal slave market located?

4. How many Africans arrived in New York between 1715 and 1740?

5. What were the plans of the substantial population of maroons in Virginia in the 1720s?

6. Why do African music and the Spiritual not translate well to the European context of music?

7. How did European warfare in the Americas help to forge the African American identity?

8. How might one compare the Spanish and British colonies to Republican and Democrat parties today?

9. In your view, how does Morgan Parker view African American identity in the context of historic struggle, in his poem "Before Revolution"?

Part Four

Summary of Part Four

Part four of *Four Hundred Souls* by Ibram X. Kendi and Keisha N. Blain moves through the transformative era of the latter half of the eighteenth century. Progress was made on behalf of Black folk, in that they became more emboldened to rebel against their masters or stand up in court and defend themselves legally.

While there were some movements made by some white folk to abolish the slave trade and delegitimize the owning of slaves, there were new ideas brought in that allowed for further ideas on why Black people could be subjugated. There were movements between further movements between the Black and Native American relationship, and we start to see Black women and preachers becoming more vocal and recognizable for their eloquence and a deep sense of spirituality.

Questions:

1. What did the Negro Act of 1740 mean for slaves?

2. What is Lucy Terry Prince best known for?

3. How did the European Enlightenment impact race relations in the Americas?

4. How did the retreat of the Spanish in 1754 impact African American and Indigenous relations?

5. For what reason did the Native American Commander Pontiac demand a Black slave from the besieged British in Detroit?

6. What was Phillis Wheatley's first published poem about?

7. How did David George leave his mark on African American history?

8. How did a lady named Mumbet turn the newly won Independence to her advantage?

9. How does Justin Phillip Reed frame his poem "Not Without Some Instances of Uncommon Cruelty"?

Part Five

Summary of Part Five

Four Hundred Souls moves into the turbulent 19th century, we look at the remnants of the Empire and how certain cities readjusted to being in a new country. We look at how Black folk sought new ways to establish their relationship with belief and religion, but also how the newfound independence of the US did not necessarily translate to independence for Black Americans.

We see how lucrative the slave trade remained how reliant many were still on slave labor. We also look at the interpersonal relationships between slaves and their owners and between each other.

Questions:

1. For what reason was Savannah founded?

2. How was the Free African Society affiliated?

3. How did Sally Hemings and Thomas Jefferson know each other?

4. What were the consequences of the Fugitive Slave Act?

5. How did the slave trade impact education in the US?

6. Who led the Louisiana Rebellion?

7. How much of the population of Louisiana were enslaved?

8. Why is studying the history of African American queerness a challenging task?

9. How does Ishmael Reed present trial and execution in his poem "Remembering the Albany"?

Part Six

Summary of Part Six

As Ibram X. Kendi and Keisha N. Blain take us into the mid 19th century in *Four Hundred Souls* we begin to see greater and greater mobilizations of Black folk. The frustrations of many African Americans spilled out into action, in some cases violent and desperate.

But in other cases, Black identity was emerging as a strong and passionate voice. Despite the best efforts of white authorities, many Black folks began to publish and speak publicly. Regardless of the challenges presented by legislation and white anxiety, many took their place in society as business owners or doctors and sought education and self-improvement to lift themselves out of servitude.

Questions:

1. How was Denmark Vesey's plotted revolution thwarted?

2. What was the purpose of *Freedom's Journal*?

3. What were Maria Stewart's frustrations with Black men?

4. What was one of the major outcomes of the National Negor Conventions?

5. How did George Latimer elude capture?

6. Where did James McCune Smith get his doctorate?

7. What were some of the challenges facing Black business owners in 19th century Oregon?

8. How did the Dred Scott case impact the rights of African descendants to this day?

9. How does Donkia Kelly suggest Black Americans come to terms with their history in her poem "Compromise"?

Part Seven

Summary of Part Seven

As Ibram X. Kendi and Keisha N. Blain take us through the last part of the 19th century in *Four Hundred Souls* we begin to see how a post-slavery America emerged. We see characters such as Frederick Douglass mobilize the North and the first votes for Black people. Their triumphs for Blacks in America and things start to look a little like progress.

But as is so often the case with race relations in America, the more progress is made the more fierce the opposition. We see also the rise of the Ku Klux Klan who wages nothing less than a war of terror against Black people and those that support them. We see the difficulties faced by newly freed slaves and poor housing in places like Atlanta.

Questions:

1. What did Frederick Douglass advocate for as the North readied itself for war with the South?

2. When did the first election in which a Black person could vote occur?

3. How did the Kirk-Holden War end?

4. How did the Ku Klux Klan Act have an effect on Klan activities?

5. Who were the biggest demographic of workers in Atlanta in the 1870s?

6. What were the demands of the Indemnity Party?

7. Why was there an outpouring of support for Annie Cutler after she shot her boyfriend dead?

8. What was the name of the newspaper run by Ida B Wells?

9. How did the Plessy v. Ferguson case affect the politics of segregation?

Part Eight

Summary of Part Eight

In this eighth part of *Four Hundred Souls,* we begin to see a more recognizable America with greater autonomy for African Americans. We see a thriving political and cultural community that was able to travel to better prospects and make a huge impact on the world stage.

But there were no fewer difficulties faced as the twentieth century drew on. Economic hardship informed political and cultural decisions and there remained those who sought to undermine Black progress and those who sought to diminish triumphs any way they could.

Questions:

1. What was the title given to Booker T Washington's historic address?

2. Which well-known novelist coined the term 'Great White Hope' and to what was he referring?

3. Which important African American institution was founded in 1909?

4. What prompted the Great Migration?

5. What factors contributed to the "Red Summer" of 1919?

6. Which revolutionary Black writers emerged from the Harlem Renaissance?

7. Why did the Communist Party hold significance for rights campaigner Angelo Herndon?

8. How long did it take Zora Neale Huston to write *Their Eyes Were Watching God*?

9. Whose messages does Patricia Smith evoke in her prose poem "Coiled and Unleashed"?

Part Nine

Summary of Part Nine

This part of *Four Hundred Souls* begins at the start of World War two and looks at the mobilization of Black soldiers against another form of white tyranny. At home, politicized left-wing Black activists face their own difficulties, and the decades-long fight to have Black kids in public school commences.

Young people are mobilized and stage their own protest and we see the rise of the Black Power movement. At a governmental level, the powers that be are beginning to look at ways to enfranchise the Black vote, but still allow opportunists to take advantage of the vulnerabilities in the Black community. We also begin to see combined movements of Black activism and feminism, drawing inspiration from early female rights campaigners.

Questions:

1. What did the blinding of Isaac Woodward contribute to?

2. What happened at Peekshill, New York in 1949?

3. What did the Brown v. Board of Education rule on May 17, 1954?

4. What was the name of the important individual who helped to mobilize student activists after the Greensboro sit-ins?

5. Who coined the term 'Black Power' and why?

6. How did the Housing and Urban Development Act of 1968 exploit vulnerable Black families and leave a legacy which would contribute to the 2008 global financial crisis?

7. Which 19th-century rebel inspired the Combahee River Collective?

8. What series of events prompted the Combahee River Collective to put out a pamphlet that interrogated sexual and racial violence against women?

9. What early twentieth-century record inspired Chet'la Sebree's poem "And the Record Repeats"?

Part Ten

Summary of Part Ten

As *Four Hundred Souls* comes to a close, we take a look back at the last forty years and how successive administrations have had often damaging effects on Black communities. We've seen how the War on Drugs backfired and had a disproportionate effect on poor Black people, and how the Clinton administration ruined the rehabilitation faculty of the US prison system.

In the 2000s we've seen the inadequate responses to Hurricane Katrina and how, after centuries of struggle, it is still possible for a Black voter to be turned away from the polling booth. We've also seen the troubling re-emergence of white nationalism. But we've also seen solidarity and support from the Black community for all women and Black culture become not only acceptable but enticing to white audiences.

Questions:

1. What did Reagan's 'War on Drugs' ultimately lead to?

2. What movement did Eric B and Rakim draw their inspiration from?

3. How many women put their name to an ad in support of Anita Hill?

4. What were the effects of Bill Clinton's Violent Crime and Law Enforcement Act?

5. What is the name of the Liberian immigrant shot dead by police officers on the 4th February 1999?

6. How did the aftermath of Hurricane Katrina disproportionately affect Black women?

7. How is it still possible for Black voters to remain disenfranchised?

8. What did the Shelby Ruling allow that could be used to keep Black people from voting?

9. What was a common feature of the perpetrators of mass shootings under the Trump administration?

Conclusion

We hope you have found the information contained in *Four Hundred Souls* or our *Summary and Analysis* of *Four Hundred Souls* by Ibram X. Kendi and Keisha N. Blain enlightening and useful. Hopefully, this workbook will have aided your reading of the books and supported your understanding of the themes in the book.

Also, make sure to purchase companion book Summary of Four Hundred Souls by Genius Reads on Amazon

Thank You!

Hope you've enjoyed your reading experience.

We here at Genius Reads will always strive to deliver to you the highest quality guides.

So, I'd like to thank you for supporting us and reading until the very end.

Before you go, would you mind leaving us a review on Amazon?

It will mean a lot to us and support us in creating high-quality guides for you in the future.

Warmly yours,

The **Genius Reads** Team

Made in the USA
Middletown, DE
12 February 2022